# The Gentleman's

# Guide

# to the

# Golden Age of

# Blowjobs

A proper thanks to my friend

Aaron Long-Jordan

*Never a question he won't answer about a big*

*ole Cock!*

# Forward

Hummer, head, BJ, even blowy or gummy. Its a blowjob, let's not beat around the bush. Now is the golden age of the blowjob! Accepted socially and a part of most relationships, the blowjob is thought to be solely on the shoulders of the "blower". I am here to tell you, this is not the case. A true gentleman must know how to receive a blowjob properly or risk being embarrassed or worse.

Without a proper understanding of the etiquette of being blown, a man could be ridiculed, left hanging, or even slapped and forgotten by his lady.

So grab a scotch, settle down next to the fire and light yourself a cigar. Lets learn how to properly receive - a blowjob.

# 1.

## Cleanliness and Grooming

Lets dive right in, Gents. The blowjob is a very intimate and sensual act which involves your significant other putting your manhood into their mouth.

Take a moment to let that sink in. In their mouth. That means they taste it, so you need to be clean. It is never going to go unappreciated if you take a pre-oral shower. Make sure to use soap and water and a light scrub. Ensure you rinse off 100% of that. Soap tastes horrible. Wash it twice if you've had a hard workout prior to the shower.

Even when you don't have time or opportunity to take a shower before oral, you can at least be a gentleman and turn down oral if you know you are sweaty or dirty. You can even allow the shower itself to be foreplay. Everyone can benefit from some help in the shower and it is a great opportunity to enjoy their body anyway.

*Let's talk about hair down there. Shall we?*

Hair down there is a touchy subject, so i am going to give you advice that most women will agree with. Bald is just as bad as long. No one wants to feel like they are having their way with a Ken Doll. You may think it looks bigger when you're bad but trust me, it doesn't.

So leave it long then? Well, no. Multi-tasking is efficient, flossing with a member in your mouth is not however enjoyable. Aside from that, who wants to feel like they need a machete to go down south? No-one.

What do i do then?! Well the middle ground is the good ground. Groom yourself down there. Cut it down a bit. Any time someone can look at a big throbbing rod and the landscape seems maintained, they will be much happier to explore it.

How short should i go? Well there are a few books out there that go over proper male grooming so go pick one of those up. Here i will just say, get it looking groomed, maintained and maybe even styled.

Try to groom every time you shower. Look at your garden and ask yourself, "Does it look like i care about this lawn?" If the answer is no and the weeds are starting to get unruly, go at it again. A simple pair of grooming scissors is the best tool in your manscaping toolbox.

# 2.

## How to ask

How do you ask for some downtown action? Well, it is important to understand that most people do not enjoy giving a gummer. Some do but they are few and far between. Never expect that someone is going to take the trip just because you want it. As i said before, blowjobs are intimate and not to be taken lightly. Therefore, asking for some slobber down under needs to be done right as not to ruin the mood.

The head nudge. We all know it. You slightly nudge their head toward your baby factory. I am here to tell you, people sit around and laugh at you for doing this. Pushing their head down is the least tactful way to request what you're after. You're not fooling anyone. On the subject of tactless, asking flat out for someone to slob on your knob is right out. It is the least gentlemanly thing you can do.

With that passed, how do you actually ask? Well that is harder to answer. You must asses the situation and roll with it. Anything worth doing is worth doing right. Maybe the foreplay is going good and you can make a comment. Maybe it's been a bad day and they want to make it better for you. Never expect it will just be given freely.

# 3.

## DO NOTS!

I'm going to give you this list of things not to do and hope you are smart enough to listen. Any time you are getting some head, your behavior is being scrutinized. There is nothing else to do down there but notice what's going on upstairs.

### Don't move your hips!

Unless we are talking about someone who has expressed an interest in you having sex with their mouth, stay still. There is a gag reflex there and your partner is doing a lot of things with their mouth. No one wants their dingdong to be scraped, bitten, or thrown up on. Right?

## Don't shut up.

Silence is not golden in this instance. How does your partner know how good they are doing without your input? Let them know if it is great! Moan a little, breathe heavy, tell them it is wonderful, call to your God, whatever works but do not be silent. Right along with this, don't stare. How awkward do you think it is when they are looking at your chest and they take a moment to look up and your "OH" face is just staring down at them. Look at them on and off but do not just stare down like you are judging them.

**Keep your hand off their head and back.**

When you put your hand on their head, you will be tempted to push their head. That is tantamount to stuffing your pole down their throat and that is not pleasant (unless they are into it).

Along with that, think about how your dad used to rub your back. Do you honestly want your partner to think about that same image with you in their mouth? I imagine you dont, so don't try to rub their back. If you need a place to put your hands, try the back of your own head.

## Don't open the floodgates without warning!

There are so many things that go go wrong if you let your swimmers loose without warning. Maybe your partner throws up at the taste. Maybe they just hate it. All men are probably guilty of this at one point or another but let's not look at the past. Something as small as improper tongue placement may cause problems that are hard to recover from romantically (I.e. The angry white dragon!).

A simple little warning is easy and wont be unwelcome. Besides, sometimes it is more fun to let the pearls fly somewhere besides in a mouth.

## Don't hold out.

Holding out on your flute player is not a great idea. I know you are probably having a wonderful time but try to be relatively brief. Time stops when you've got a member in your mouth. A minute feels like 10 and 10 feels like a day. Do not sign up for the minute men right away but also, do not attempt to make this into an hour long event. Try for a few minutes and then move on to another activity.

# 4.

## DO!

Here are some things never to forget to do. Always try to go down this checklist in your head and make sure you've covered all these bases. If you do, passing this base and sliding into the next will be all the more rewarding.

**Drink water.**

Water will help with consistency of the baby gravy. On top of being good for your body, proper hydration will give you an edge over the other guys in the taste department.

# Eat the right things!

These foods will improve your flavor.

- Pineapple
- Bananas
- Papaya
- Oranges
- Cinnamon
- Peppermint
- Nutmeg
- Parsley
- Wheatgrass
- Celery

I doubt you could get an award for tasting good, but you can at least be better than most! Better is always better.


**Reciprocate.**

It is never a bad idea to reciprocate. If your spouse is nice enough to funnel your hog, go ahead and do your own part. No one likes to feel unappreciated. Take the initiative and go south of their border. You wont regret it.

**Make the right eye contact.**

Looking down at the right moment will undoubtedly give you a great view and give them a great opportunity to enjoy your face, momentarily.

Know when to look away, however. Do not hold that eye contact forever. Go back to looking at the ceiling and praising them for their hard work.


**Stay away from certain things.**

There are specific things that will make you taste worse. You never want to be the guy who tasted like "that". I am not saying cut these things out completely but do try to cut back a bit.

Stay away from these and you will not be disappointed.

- Cigarettes
- Caffeine
- Red meat
- Onions
- Garlic

**Hold your gas.**

It pains me to have to say this. If it seems like it is going to work its way out, excuse yourself. Literally telling them that your stomach is upset is better than blowing that horn just inches from their face.

# 5.

## Short Tips & Tricks

- Nothing says "i'm not coming back" like a boring BJ. Let your partner know that you appreciate it. Kiss all over the place, touch everywhere, trace shapes on their skin.

- Hair is hard to clean. Try not to get any of your special sauce in hair. It is tough to get out. If mistakes are made and something does happen, vinegar will help to clean it out. Knowing this will save the day and make you a proper gentleman in the moment.

- If you're going to do it, do it. Don't leave clothes on, if they like you enough to get down and dirty then they want to look at you. Let your hair down and let your colors fly. Get naked, make it fun.
- Don't make it awkward. You're already here, never let it be awkward. Smile, whisper, and be a gentleman without letting embarrassment even cross your mind.

# Afterward

I wanted to take a bit here to discuss fetishes and fun. Everyone likes a little fetish or two and these are not to be shunned. There are those who very much enjoy taking a good hard jackhammer to the throat, for insance.

Always remember to communicate prior to getting yourself a blowy and let these topics "come up" on their own. If your partner actually prefers a pearl mask to a pearl necklace or a protein shot, let them bring it up.

The other side of this coin is, if you prefer to steam truck into their tonsils, ask about it. This conversation has to be treated a lot like the first date conversation. Risk and reward are the name of the game. The worst that can happen is they say "No" and the best is they say "Yes". How you get to those answers is however not irrelevant.

Always be polite and a gentleman, this is not "The Rapscallions Guide to Getting a $5 Knocker Jockey in an Ally" this is a gentleman's guide and as such, always present yourself in a gentlemanly manner.

Scotch helps.

Printed in Great Britain
by Amazon

31253921R00020